I0798919

Lynda Monahan

A BEAUTIFUL STONE

Poems and Ululations

Rod Thompson

Cover art: Kim Ennis
Book and cover design: Tania Wolk, Third Wolf Studio
Printed and bound in Canada at Friesens, Altona, MB

The publisher gratefully acknowledges the support of Creative Saskatchewan and the Saskatchewan Arts Board.

creative SASKATCHEWAN

SINCE 1948 SASKATCHEWAN ARTS BOARD

Library and Archives Canada Cataloguing in Publication

Title: A beautiful stone : poems and ululations / Lynda Monahan, Rod Thompson.
Names: Monahan, Lynda, 1952- author. | Thompson, Rod (Rodney Lee), 1952- author.
Identifiers: Canadiana (print) 20190159561 |
Canadiana (ebook) 20190159588 |
ISBN 9781989274200 (softcover) | ISBN 9781989274217 (PDF)
Subjects: LCGFT: Poetry.
Classification: LCC PS8576.O45182 B43 2019 | DDC C811/.54—dc23

radiant press
Box 33128 Cathedral PO
Regina, SK S4T 7X2
info@radiantpress.ca
www.radiantpress.ca

"A thousand things up and down the street, deep, lovely, dangerous, aureating, breathing, throbbing like stars; a whistle; a faint yell; the bark on the river; the wild goose of the night yakking, ducking in the sand and sparkle; the ululating lap and purl and lovely mystery on the shore..."

—*Jack Kerouac*

CHOICE OF LIGHT

LOON AND I

ULULATION

CHOICE OF LIGHT

Cadence

Years ago, I canoed places few have ventured,
mapped daily progress, rose early to make
the day's miles. an apprentice, my one task to run
the bellows, to keep that steady rhythm
of breath and lung song.

Now, with the watery Everests behind me,
the point is one stroke after the next,
the entry, pull, exit, again, then again.
No yardsticks need mark the day.

Just the cadence of push and pull,
the satisfaction of fanning the flames
as the wild world whispers and sings.

Choice of Light

Something about the night, so much softer
than the day's hard glare. I love its depth,
memories drifting like fireflies, the spill
of moonlight on the cool grass.

Holding a candle above your lover
is a choice now, a delicate way
to leave a day crowded
with light-emitting diodes
casting sharp shadows
on multiple ways to stay in touch.

The blare of traffic behind
the chattering newscaster
from the always-on tv
as again, we turn away from the sun,
reaching for a switch,
our instincts moaning with the wolves.

Following the Way

We wander the trail, talking family, stopping to touch
the bark of balsam, taste low bush cranberries.

What is it about love, we wonder, why does it hold
such hurt? We are like the geese, always on our way

to breeding grounds or a safe wintering place, always
following the way, bound and together, mindful of deadfall.

We gather moss for stone egg nests, carry them home,
our journeys end - foul weather or fair, always home.

His Last Eden

the door itself makes no promises
it is only a door
–Adrienne Rich
(from *Prospective Migrants Please Note*)

Great grandfather went into things
not knowing what he was going to get,
always searching for the next quarter section,
a place more fertile, with more room and hope,
a base for the children to begin their quests
far from the scars of that damn war
and his hard scrabble childhood.

In his last Eden, exhausted and alone,
with a pistol to his head,
the reason he opened the door
was because it was just a door,
and he wanted whatever was behind it -
the first place with no promises.

His life's quest feeling like a long long run,
he took his chances, he took that step.

Inheritance

I wish I had a grandmother's hug kind of heart,
a plush cushion made of real red velvet,
the kind that takes you to the grocery store
for a romance novel
while others hunt for milk and sirloin.

Or the practical sort,
pillowy and useful as a feather tick
after a long day walking wide open spaces,
a resting place without phones or lists,
clean and cottony as a summer cloud.

Instead of this rickety uncle,
this spindle-backed naked
old aching kind of heart
that runs from others
to a shack trapping sage brush.

Of Fish and Fiddleheads

One warm spring day,
out in my new Starcraft Cruiser,
I gathered pickerel from the lake
where I knew they waited just off Prospect Point

and later we stopped on the road to the Narrows.
You stood lookout for park wardens
while I, with shovel over my shoulder,
tromped into the forest to dig fiddleheads.

I'm not one to boast,
I'm no native, but it feels so good
to step out of the can of winter,
hand you a plate of wild white and green

to nourish ourselves,
with the promise of tender days.

Questions for a True Night Sky

Under a true night sky far from here, we
arrive knowing our families, their tragedies.

Are we stronger sharing Orion with the Greeks,
the North Star with the Vikings, smoke wrapping
our faces, wreathing up from our mouths
softening the air around us?

Are we the bravest of explorers without the names
and stories that sheltered our elders under
a true night sky, will we find our way to the end
of days, flames flickering at our wrists?

Are we less alone calling the stars by name?
We are the ones who taste their sharpness,
the peat fires of our hearts burning in the night.

Rituals Burnished

Confined to the house, grandfather took comfort
knowing that out there in the workshop
each tool was sharp and up in the beams
fresh blocks of larch were drying,
chips swept from the plank floor,
each chisel and mallet within easy reach.

Once a week grandfather paid me fifty cents
to polish his boots. Winter nights in the easy chair
in the glow of his easy stories, I'd open
the old red shoeshine box, small flat tins of Kiwi polish
and carefully folded shammies. I loved the smell
of the wax, the way the boots worked
up to a fine gleam as I rubbed the paste
into the soft leather.

I'd line them up outside his bedroom door
so they'd be there for him come morning
when he'd hand me the fifty cents.
I can see my face in these boots
he'd tell me and I'd walk away smiling, paid in full.

Stories for His Funeral

He gave his grandson
the high points for his eulogy:
the wonder in that whale's eye,
deer at the lip of the clearing,
the Leicester City miracle,

the record trout and the song
of the river that day
he saw a skim of crimson fox
in the soft mouth of the wind.

Forgiveness for the times
he was like autumn fires,
all wood smoke and longing.

His grandson insists
the best stories are about the kayak
he bought when grandma was away,
the hundred dollars he lost
betting the grandchildren
they couldn't guess a football score.

Storm Stayed

Snow splintering the headlights, we arrive
at last and for three days schedules
are cancelled, bookings missed while we watch
white cotton unfurl outside our window
into a thick deep quilt wrapped all around us.

Home is the snug cave we do not venture from,
power out, we forage together
sharing stories never told before, huddled
in the firelight, we listen to nature howl and dance
over the absurdity of our frail goals and deadlines,
so far away.

Taste of Childhood

Grandma filled the kitchen Sunday mornings
with the smell of biscuits pulled from the oven, crusty
on the outside, soft inside, warm whiteness
stained with choke-cherry syrup

made from berries hung like jewels where Grandpa
and I picked them along the river, smooth stones
and sun, long afternoons drowsy with bees,
the two of us puckering with purple smiles.

We ate as many biscuits as it took
for grandma to know we needed her.

LOON AND I

Glances

Rosemary
the long ago girlfriend
you once loved -
I don't even try
to get it to grow

dust settles
on the gravel road,
my lips -
you left quickly
car so sleek so clean

runnels
of rain slipping down
the windowpane
your fingers tracing my face
in the watery light

this freeway
once a path
this city, a village
our romance
a glance

scent of rain
on parched soil
something you released in me
an essence
earth perfume

Loon and I

black and white
photo of families
at the beach
moms in rubber swim caps
not a jetboat in sight

best hiking trip?
two days of rain
tapping the tent
us in sleeping bags
deck of cards between us

perfectly happy
when the power goes out
at the cabin
I light coal oil lanterns
read in the flickering light

what risk
taking these long days
for ourselves
hike up to that little lake
carve wooden boats

feeling selfish
I say no to the long list
of obligations
pack my bags for a week
spent on my own

back again
on this rocky shore
a loon and I
her sunset song
combing my tangled thoughts

Mother

standing there
in this sepia photo
she is still as a deer
at the road's edge
we hardly see her at all

who inherits
all her ceramic roosters,
farmyard toughs
frightening little girls
running to the barn

the surprise
of marsh marigolds
she loved
not petunias lined up
in rows like small soldiers

two sisters
their families faltering
over condolences,
choice of urn,
how well she loved

picking berries
her wedding ring
slipped from my finger
all these years later
I find myself searching

On the Potter's Wheel

write a decent poem
in every coffee shop -
a retirement goal
that separates me
from the old loners

writing
late into the night
at the cabin
I curve into
these slow hours

pencils
stacked like cordwood
on the desk,
now if only this one
would catch fire

who writes these poems?
not I   this incendiary
tall flick of a woman
casting the heat of her words
into the dark of old nights

some poems
fall from the sky,
wet ice crystals
interlaced
melting

some poems
are frozen clouds

of breath
my pen
is blue ivory

few people
at the poetry reading,
one of them
head between her knees
whispering to a phone

travelled
winter roads six hours
to the reading
sold one copy
to the town librarian

lump of clay
on the potters wheel
cup bowl vase?
no wrong way
yet still I'm frightened

On This Road

if only
his way was smooth
and easy
not half the road under water
whole sections closed

since returning home
I avoid the phone -
telling well-wishers
only what they
need to hear

the tattoo on his wrist
reads family
covers scars
of where he cut, years of pain
not hidden by that word

years of depression
were never friends
just vagrants
lost in the crowd
holding my coins

help me
to know how to be
with you
I am as lost on this road,
dear one, as you

One More Winter

snow in tatters
dry grass bent
to the rising sun -
father a twig
willing the buds to flush

the thing
with grizzly bears
is to keep clear -
father even in dying
huffing at us to leave him be

morning bowel movement
sun room nap after lunch
a good day
like golfing in Hawaii
the smell of a new car

nothing better
than a roast beef dinner
and a couple of beers -
I spoon feed him milk pudding
mouth wide as a baby bird's

in the nursing home
immigrant caregivers
keep father alive
their names in his pocket
a small book of unfamiliar sounds

finally
running out of himself
so little left
the few remaining crumbs
the last speckle of salt

stumbling again
into the holes
in his memory
he asks
did I treat your mother well?

Partners

paper birch
line the lakeshore -
you wrote me a small poem
on a strip of bark
the night my father died

you crept away
before breakfast
leaves falling
sunlight and dew
partners for a time

grieving,
my good friend
has lost her father too -
I give her a journal
to write sorrow in

old cabin
mossy logs softening
but for a small mirror
hanging squarely
in the curve of time

evening
enters the forest
quietly
two old companions
trees and time

the day's cuttings
composting in the garden
robin pulling worms -
one thing into another
even the stars

Pull

I follow the river
downstream
like a pickerel
netted by the quiet pull
of sun and open water

this yard needs
a pond with lilies,
a hungry koi
and a shaded place to sit -
back to the endless prairie

a small fox
crosses the current-
flame bright
the river becomes
the animal, softly furred

this morning
in last year's leaf
last night's rain,
enough for a picture
enough for this thirsty traveler

a wink
inside a waterdrop
cellophane wings
of dragonflies
moments we are here

Ripples

tall young birch
the colour of otter bone
beginning to green -
my slender grandsons
with their first whiskers

his first
stone into a pond,
so round
so many ripples,
the need to repeat

deer, fox
red willow, river pine
this forest
these poems circling
back again to home

granddaughter
testing the depth
of spring,
meltwater rushing
again into her boots

brother and I raced
baking soda boats
in the stream -
now only I am
left to remember

Run of Sun and Shadow

glass –
seems a shame
to ripple it
sliding this canoe
into the sunrise

flotilla
of fishing boats
on the horizon -
flat bottom clouds
moored to the sky

paddling
this prairie reservoir
waves prancing -
white horses
nudging my kayak

the run
of sun and shadow
bright sails
catching the wind -
my boat learning to fly

tides massage
this marriage of land and water,
tethered skiff
as at home in muck
as the pulsing sea

Sanctuary

each morning
tooth brush mumble
affirmations taped to the mirror
shaving next to
"Each day is a gift"

my french milled soap
apple scented body butter
cinnabar perfume
his nail clippers
toothbrush and comb

one last time
neck-tie cinched
deep breath
face the mirror
give him the speech

door locked
perched on the toilet seat
sobbing
  into a bath towel
  so no one can hear

three generations
stepped from the day's rush
into this tub,
an iron relic
on lion's-claw feet

Time to Waste

simple gift
this sweat-soaked day,
bees and bluebells
to take away
winter's thickness

power out
no way to cook supper -
a merlot
cinnamon scented candles
and a picnic on the grass

our tidy
square linen space
on the forest floor
where ants and bears
may want to share

sultry night
white sheets of lightning
hanging
on the thin line
of a dark horizon

axe
wedged in a stump,
angle jaunty
blue bells dangling
over stillness

sky fall
lake mirroring
the stars,
moon raking a path
from the breakwater

hours
on this stump
carving
a rake handle
I could buy in minutes

ladyslipper
hidden in the grass
at the road's edge -
some gifts are hard to see
yet they are still there

jobless now
this damsel fly
can take his time
warming himself
on my knee

Winter's Window

this red head
banging my eaves trough
so brash
so territorial
so woodpecker

old raccoon
raiding the birdfeeder
helping himself -
grandpa taking the last
of the mashed potatoes

a rigid sparrow
lies on the deck,
another window victim -
the cat pushes it aside
to hunt for prey

coyote calls me
to the snow moon
outside my window -
a shiver of hoarfrost
settles to the ground

a mouse shuffles
under the snow -
the moonlight
on the owl's talons
released

ULULATION

Aftershock

it was a secret
she promised not to tell-
a week later
their forty-year friendship over

the way an earthquake
makes rubble
out of everything

HAPPY BIRTHDAY DAD
taped to each wall -
bubbly in one hand, whisky in the other
he toasts us all

the way an earthquake
makes rubble
out of everything

that late night
phone call
the tremble of tears
in her son's voice

the way an earthquake
makes rubble
out of everything

just you and I smothered
under a snow day
talking, feeding the fire -
until the county plow arrives

the way an earthquake
makes rubble
out of everything

that single word
suicide
with all its aftershocks
these many years later

the way an earthquake
makes rubble
out of everything

The Asbestos Forest

lightning strikes
to the south east-
a deep throated rumble
the sky boils darkness

I'm the asbestos forest
that never burns

she braced herself
against the first question -
this young therapist insisting
sharing would help

I'm the asbestos forest
that never burns

like the spruce by the river
a strip of bark
struck from her breast -
a scar she wears, a medallion

I'm the asbestos forest
that never burns

she crams so much into the margins
between crossed out words -
his notes are tidy
tiny letters in obedient lines

I'm the asbestos forest
that never burns

such a good girl, everyone said
looking after her motherless family-
little sister throwing tantrums
her brother failing in school

I'm the asbestos forest
that never burns

The Best Light

chanting with my mighty tribe
for justice from the referee -
love and hate in righteous waves
another year victory waits

feeling for candles
in the dark
my power gone

at the conference
the edgy young writer
with her power point presentation
has all the audience

feeling for candles
in the dark
my power gone

bought two fishing rods online
the ones for skillful fly fishers -
the elite few delivered
in a box, express to my door

feeling for candles
in the dark
my power gone

I savour slender volumes
of old poems   in my hands -
the Kindle my daughter-in-law
bought for my birthday

feeling for candles
in the dark
my power gone

they gather around tables
in the food court -
silent children gazing into the light
of their phones

feeling for candles
in the dark
my power gone

I miss the subtle shadows
thrown by kerosene lanterns-
softer than the cold glare
of these LED lights

feeling for candles
in the dark
my power gone

Choose the Time

all these years
sis picks up the morning puppy poo
beside the training pads-
"little gifts," she says

every one searches
best they can
some more grateful than others

my sister weeps
at the beauty of this day
as we gather beach glass
I worry for tomorrow

every one searches
best they can
some more grateful than others

mother said the neighbor boy
who hung himself
failed to try hard enough
cutting her grass

every one searches
best they can
some more grateful than others

so quiet at the lake
this time of year   my friend calls
says she just couldn't wait
to get out of there

every one searches
best they can
some more grateful than others

sharing old times father always chose
the year his mother died
and sis burned the house down
and the beatings began

every one searches
best they can
some more grateful than others

The Delicate Balance of Two

end of the dock   end of the day
only a loon speaks
as the wilderness sets
between us

on the edge
the rhythmic shuffle
of beach pebbles

perched on a rock
the blue heron waits -
there is no hurry
only the tell of time

on the edge
the rhythmic shuffle
of beach pebbles

we walk past the canoe rental sign-
today only memories offer
graceful lines
the delicate balance of two

on the edge
the rhythmic shuffle
of beach pebbles

the low sun
glinting the water-
to think you are somewhere
struck by the same light

on the edge
the rhythmic shuffle
of beach pebbles

40
41

Fragilities

a chickadee wheels hard
into my kitchen window -
I carry its silence
lay it gently on the snow

after the earthquake
children gather the stained glass
amongst the cathedral stones

hunched over by the frosted window
her arthritic paint-stained hands
creating deer and children
on a green hill with happy trees

after the earthquake
children gather the stained glass
amongst the cathedral stones

from twigs and leaves
stones and snow
his creations refined by nature
sculpted by wind and rain

after the earthquake
children gather the stained glass
amongst the cathedral stones

outside this truck
a bare face would in minutes
look like the moon
lighting these empty fields

after the earthquake
children gather the stained glass
amongst the cathedral stones

dusk- colored fawn
born late in the season
as the first snow arrives -
survival sparked with hope

after the earthquake
children gather the stained glass
amongst the cathedral stones

the snow falls this day
on the snow of yesterdays
quiet crystal tangles wait
for their run to the sea

after the earthquake
children gather the stained glass
amongst the cathedral stones

From Below

bioluminescence -
those things
that make their own light
inside her like lantern fish

riding up
from the sightless depths
at dusk

screen door slams
against the insistent day -
so much I should do
before that ragged boy arrives

riding up
from the sightless depths
at dusk

that little lump
she tells me
might be grief bubbling up
since its above your heart

riding up
from the sightless depths
at dusk

so many miles -
proper shoes and training
to keep pace with friends -
in the long run   stillness

riding up
from the sightless depths
at dusk

he believes soft
is a woman thing -
part of him learned
long ago not to let anyone see

riding up
from the sightless depths
at dusk

father's family hardened
on generations of stony soil
losing sons to war
and always the rage

riding up
from the sightless depths
at dusk

Hiking

hiking through another's poem
pen in hand, I leave marks
to show I've been there
that I shared or could not.

a beautiful stone
is more so
when touched

locked out
of a closed door poem -
ringing the bell
but there is no answer

a keyhole
I peep through -
one small window in

a few join me in the library
sifting through slim volumes
on the sale table
for words to touch

most hunt for them
in greeting cards before
a birthday   after a death

six bookshelves
crammed to overflowing
with prize-winning titles
from the best sellers list

the poem I can't forget -
graffiti
underneath the bridge

the best art is useful
like chert or flint   everything
not needed to hunt and to cut
knapped away

your poem
hurt -
so small   so polished

a wide deep river
of dark currents and swells
hidden boulders
and dangerous undertows

art is
to breathe
with the flow of the water

across the lake
a wolf's howl
chases a loon's laugh
from the day

me with a pencil
and journal
trying to participate

Holding On

my friend writes all will be well
and I know
the truth of that -
but when and how?

alone at the granite face
reaching for climbing chalk
and faith

each year fewer friends
gather at the beach -
summers first fire
now cold by dawn

alone at the granite face
reaching for climbing chalk
and faith

after the diagnosis
he flutters around her
like a frightened bird
bringing tea and blankets

alone at the granite face
reaching for climbing chalk
and faith

this government expert
as tasteless as the lead in our water
charts the risks and probabilities
for our child's future

alone at the granite face
reaching for climbing chalk
and faith

his mother dying
the boy wants to shatter
to see something in shards
though he isn't sure what

alone at the granite face
reaching for climbing chalk
and faith

forty years since our baby left
no time then for the sobs
that force their way
into the quiet of my golden years

alone at the granite face
reaching for climbing chalk
and faith

this roadmap to loss
and pain -
what does it mean
to be the last one standing?

alone at the granite face
reaching for climbing chalk
and faith

Last Paddle

they were the first
to rise with the loons
and the sun
touching the tree tops

her gift
a canoe paddle
painted on his urn

every autumn they canoed
the Bladebone route -
string of little lakes
hills of orange and gold

her gift
a canoe paddle
painted on his urn

they loved beneath a sky
that flattened land and water
into a thin pale line
under the sweep of possibility

her gift
a canoe paddle
painted on his urn

glimpses and ripples
of laughter
and a tumble of otters
alongside their canoe

her gift
a canoe paddle
painted on his urn

their whole world
between the gunnels
packed to fit on their backs-
home a portage away

her gift
a canoe paddle
painted on his urn

before breakfast
they'd be afloat
on the perfection
of a summer morning

her gift
a canoe paddle
painted on his urn

as the years pass
and the stories swell
the bones know
the last portage is near

her gift
a canoe paddle
painted on his urn

Mint Summers

summer is too short
to waste gardening
except for watching the children
steal the strawberries

I shall wait here
for the sun
behind that pine

wild mint
deep in the forest -
the river a window
into patterns of light

I shall wait here
for the sun
behind that pine

morning ritual –
finger tips hunt
tender quack grass stems
beneath the carrot tops

I shall wait here
for the sun
behind that pine

a gift of sunflower seeds
for the gang of chickadees
chasing the air
around my shoulders

I shall wait here
for the sun
behind that pine

Story

two days left of January's
snow and wind and brittle branches -
February, the sun will climb
for us   but not for father

this is my story
the best I can shape
for me   for you

two days into February
morning snow glitters
like his last Christmas tree
so recently abandoned in the back yard

this is my story
the best I can shape
for me   for you

I could have been an artist
working words and wood
shown father another way -
to build a shameless day

this is my story
the best I can shape
for me   for you

I could have been a dancer-
a white curve a sail
against the wind
of father's anger

this is my story
the best I can shape
for me   for you

without the north wind
or the sanctuary of home,
where to rest
what to push against

this is my story
the best I can shape
for me   for you

without that grey bluster
I listen for soft laughter -
the low sun's leaving
the child I was to smile at me

this is my story
the best I can shape
for me   for you

Ululation

her heart speaks
the language of loon -
understands
that ancient lullaby

listen
to the rise and fall
that distant ululation

end of the dock
lid off his ashes
harder than she thought
facing a cold wind   letting go

listen
to the rise and fall
that distant ululation

in winter
the loon's song is silent
yet in me still
as his last breath

listen
to the rise and fall
that distant ululation

on this brittle winter day
the long rhythmic wail
of each traveler
on the distant highway

listen
to the rise and fall
that distant ululation

his voice is memory -
wind song
through the pines
on winter nights

listen
to the rise and fall
that distant ululation

the city of my youth
pulses on the horizon
all spires and allure
beyond the prairie roses

listen
to thc rise and fall
that distant ululation

trudge through snow
boot deep to the bridge -
memories restless as the river
beneath its blanket of ice

listen
to the rise and fall
that distant ululation

Visiting Father

lunch at the Steakhouse
afternoon by the river
supper sipping soup
in front of game seven

so many years
before we waste
a day together

he insisted on
turkey dinner all the trimmings
rolled oat stuffing
for every occasion

last Christmas
his request
a small bowl of rice pudding

list of steps taped to the computer -
the third version -
each shorter
each harder to follow

the tools that hung in his shop
now in boxes
priced to sell

all dressed up on Saturday nights -
out dancing at the Suburban Inn
drinking rye and coke
until closing time

lately in bed by ten
too tired to stay up
for the evening news

shuffling past neighbors
never a look or wave
as they are hoisted into their day chairs -
travelers on another train

waiting for breakfast
table mates, servers, everyone
holding on for better days

again for the last time
into the fresh air
from the hallways and ticking clocks
and heads on chests

he'd run too
if he could drive
and remember where

We Cannot Know

cardiac ablation risks:
puncture of the heart
blood clots in the lungs
stroke or in rare cases death

all the what if's
throwing fuel
on the fire of my worry

squeezed into an old suit jacket
and job interview room
trying to explain the blank years
why nothing for hobbies

all the what if's
throwing fuel
on the fire of my worry

depression passed on
in our family
like the darkness
of our eyes

all the what if's
throwing fuel
on the fire of my worry

in the crowded coffee shop
I should have offered her my table
proposed we share a morning biscuit
for the rest of our lives

all the what if's
throwing fuel
on the fire of my worry

Weathered

I should carve a new hoe handle
easier still   buy another -
instead   I'll rub oil into weathered wood
two times   in the sun

one more season
pensionable friends in hand
purpose clear

no expensive new watercraft
boiling up the lake   stereo blaring
he rescues an old row boat   touches it
with something a lot like love

one more season
pensionable friends in hand
purpose clear

second Tuesday of each month
in the church basement -
less elders than the year before
approve the treasurers report

one more season
pensionable friends in hand
purpose clear

a great grandmother now
written on her skin
the poem of all she has weathered -
the little ones read the lines

one more season
pensionable friends in hand
purpose clear

one left
who can drive the rest
to the ice hut
they built sixty years ago

one more season
pensionable friends in hand
purpose clear

Wrapped In Stillness

my son is a good man
and his son so like him
though neither are like
this lake so smooth and still

on a sea
of breakers
and rolling desires

yellow leaves falling
into a still morning
where you sat
writing good-bye

on a sea
of breakers
and rolling desires

an island
she's never been to -
somewhere still
her distant destination

on a sea
of breakers
and rolling desires

I long still
for the safety of her dark womb -
quarter sawn tamarack   clinker joined
centuries of dreams held by craftsman

on a sea
of breakers
and rolling desires

I remember still
the day he showed me
his new tattoo   an anchor
that was meant to keep him safe

on a sea
of breakers
and rolling desires

chattering away
in our little boat of serious fishermen
ignoring our requests
to please be still

on a sea
of breakers
and rolling desires

Gifts

daughter-in-law
finds me a flicker feather-
brother-in-law   the gift
of a hummingbird's nest

small treasures
in the palm of my hand

sun rising
before the neighbours do -
chill silence
coffee mug steaming

small treasures
in the palm of my hand

late summer light
slanting through pines
wild blueberries
in a yellow bowl

small treasures
in the palm of my hand

who held
this arrow head
before we arrived
with plows and dreams

small treasures
in the palm of my hand

baby spider
rescued from the bathtub-
set him on a blade of grass
next to a drop of dew

small treasures
in the palm of my hand

horizon days away
boot laces snug
one more spring
crocus to my lips

small treasures
in the palm of my hand

grandfather's books-
I close my eyes
to imprint the texture
of old leather

small treasures
in the palm of my hand

first frost
last of the corn
time for covers
and golden threads

small treasures
In the palm of my hand

Understory

pick the cranberry
above my head
I will taste it
you will smile

this path winds through these hills for us

climb the tower
at the height of land-
Shady Lake and sun
through the tops of poplars

this path winds through these hills for us

look here   as I do
the sun sticks
to each spider thread
holding the forest together

this path winds through these hills for us

listen to the tales
of a tall white spruce-
let it tell you its understory
of honeysuckle and wild rose

this path winds through these hills for us

run in the pines
just run in the pines
let the yellow green needles
trade their breath for yours

this path winds through these hills for us

ACKNOWLEDGEMENTS

Thank you to Radiant Press for believing in the worth of this poetic adventure. We would like to express our deep appreciation to Dave Margoshes for his wisdom and insightful editing of this collection. And, as always, heartfelt thanks to our families for their generous and steadfast love.

—Lynda Monahan and Rod Thompson

Lynda Monahan

Author of three collections of poetry, A Slow Dance in the Flames, What My Body Knows, *(Coteau Books) and* Verge *(Guernica Editions). She facilitates creative writing workshops and has been writer-in-residence at St. Peter's College facilitated retreat and the Victoria Hospital in Prince Albert, Saskatchewan. She is editor of* Second Chances: *stories of brain injury survivors,* Skating in the Exit Light, *a poetry anthology, and* With Just One Reach of Hands, *an anthology of the writing of the Canadian Mental Health Association's Writing For Your Life group, which she also facilitates. She recently finished a term as writer in residence at the JM Culenaere Library in Prince Albert, Saskatchewan.*

Rod Thompson

Rod Thompson lives in the forest west of the city of Prince Albert, Saskatchewan. He has had his poetry published in a number of literary magazines including *Grain, Transition, Blue Jay* and *The Prairie Journal.* He has long enjoyed writing tanka and haiku and his tanka have been published in *American Tanka, Lynx, Tangled Hair,* and most recently in in *Atlas Poetica*, an American tanka journal.